Social-Emotional Learning: Positive-Preventive Skill Building Activities for Young Children

CONTENTS

DEDICATION

This Social-Emotional Learning series is dedicated to all the early childhood educators who work diligently to provide our youth with the social-emotional and academic skills they need to be successful in school and life.

CHAPTER 1

INTRODUCTION

Social Emotional Learning (SEL)

Young children learn by play, doing, and observing their world around them. Tailoring play to incorporate activities that promote positive social-emotional development teaches children many important behavioral and life skills, and readies them for future academic success.

Communication is the basis of all learning, both academic and behavioral, but equally important is the learning of social and emotional skills. According to kindergarten teachers in research performed by the National Academy of Sciences in 2008 only 40% of children possess the skills necessary to do well upon their arrival.

To set our children up success in school and life we need to establish a good base of functional communication. Otherwise we will see negative behavior as a result of not getting their needs met. A newborn gets our attention for things by crying in an attempt to tell us they are in need. The need may be food, a change of diaper, or simply to be held. From a communication standpoint there is a better way. We suggest the learning of sign language to teach basic signs to infants to express their needs. Long before we can talk we know what we want, we simply do not possess the vocal ability to express it. Using sign language can greatly enhance our children's ability to let us know specifically what they want or need. The children of deaf parents is taught sign language from birth. By speaking age they know on average 100 more concepts than the vocal language family's children by speaking age. As they wait until their children can speak to begin teaching them the same concepts.

As we build a firm foundation of functional communication we need to teach social and emotional skills to our children. Again, we go about this by simply adding activities that touch on these points. When we succeed in establishing a firm foundation in functional communication and teach children social-emotional skills we greatly reduce their likelihood of having behavioral and academic issues.

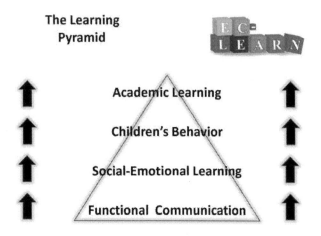

The development of young children's social-emotional knowledge and skills includes activities and strategies that promote student understanding and management of emotions, goal setting and achievement, relationship building and maintenance, problem solving, and decision making.

Students must be explicitly taught social-emotional skills.

Why is it so important to learn social and emotional skills early in life?

- Increased academic achievement
- Increased social-emotional skills
- Improved attitudes toward self and others
- Improved positive social behaviors
- Decreased behavioral problems
- Decreased emotional stress
- Improved school climate
- Increased attendance and graduation rates

🖐   Improved college and career readiness
(e.g., problem solving skills, frustration, tolerance)

According to CASEL (Collaborative for Academic, Social, and Emotional Learning), there are five social and emotional learning core competencies. They are:

1.   Self-management: Managing emotions and behaviors to achieve one's goals.
2.   Self-awareness: Recognizing one's emotions and values as well as one's strengths and challenges.
3.   Social awareness. Showing understanding and empathy for others.

4.   Responsible decision-making. Making ethical, constructive choices about personal and social behavior.

5. Relationship skills. Forming positive relationships, working in teams, dealing effectively with conflict.

It is through play that children develop friendships and seek to find the acceptance of their peers, which is how social skills are learned. Children who are socially and emotionally healthy have mastered the necessary social and emotional skills. As a result, they develop positive relationships with peers and teachers. Further, these skills have a lasting impact on academic achievement, because they contribute to more positive feelings about school, and eagerness to engage in classroom activities.

According to Child Care and Early Education Research Connections (2013), development in social and emotional learning, communication, and understanding are important to kindergarten readiness. Researchers found that 8 of the top 11 skills required for kindergarten readiness involved social-emotional influences. The top 2 skills are self-regulation and problem-solving skills. Indeed, many refer to self-control/regulation) as your super-power. Further, self-regulation levels predict school success better than cognitive skills and family background (Boyd, J., Barnett, S., Bodrova, E., Leong, D., & Gomby, D., 2005).

Management of feelings, empathy skills, problem-solving skills, and self-control help young children achieve personal growth and development, as well as academic success (Whitted, 2011, P. 13). As teachers we need to provide an atmosphere in which our children feel emotionally secure and socially connected to adults who provide nurturance and positive opportunities for learning in a warm and caring environment. Further, we need to help them, especially in the beginning of the year, as they transition from home to school, as expectations and norms may differ greatly between the home and the classroom. The classroom environment promotes collaborative learning, rather than competition, and should be a place where all children feel good about themselves and their emergent abilities. In fact, caring teachers who take the time to get to know their children and their families well have one-third less misbehaviors in the classroom than those who do not.

Persistent physical aggression, high school dropout rates, adolescent delinquency, and antisocial behavior have all been associated with early childhood conduct problems. Therefore, it is incumbent upon us as early childhood educators to do all we can to insure that children start off on the right trajectory. Further, that we work doubly hard with children and families to correct deficiencies when children are in our care, as over time the likelihood of change diminishes and takes more effort and resources. A key component to working with challenging children is getting the families on board to help facilitate the desired change. By taking the time to get to know and befriend them we set ourselves up receive their support when we need it.

The remainder of this book is dedicated to activities that promote the social and emotional learning of young children.

CHAPTER 2

CLASSROOM ACTIVITIES TO PROMOTE SOCIAL-EMOTIONAL LEARNING

Activities that Promote Long-Term Retention, Logical Thinking; and Social, Emotional, and Academic Learning

We have short-term responses to our daily schedules, sensations, thoughts, feelings, and actions. Practice makes perfect; these short-term responses in time help us to facilitate positive long-term responses. Below you will find activities that can be done in sign to promote Long-Term Retention, Logical Thinking, and SEAL.

Research shows that young children who develop in a healthy social and emotional environment, also learn better academically (SEAL). Also, by using sign language as a tool to enhance overall brain function, we can learn to rewire the brain helping our children with logical concentration, emotional regulation, positive stress release, and overall health.

Some overarching activities that

can be utilized throughout the day include the following three areas:

- 🖐 <u>Role Playing</u> -- Guide your child in how to display emotions in situations that occur. For example, when my brother takes my toy, sign and say "mommy help me" or "sharing".

- 🖐 <u>Classroom Helper</u> -- How will your helpers be chosen? What tasks would you like to select for the children to do? Count helper, clean up helper, line up leader, etc. Make a helper chart and encourage your children to sign the helper signs for their respective tasks.

- 🖐 <u>Praise</u> -- Incorporate praising words and phrases that are specific to the action being praised throughout the day to encourage and reward children for their efforts to learn, communicate, and cooperation with friends.

Stories

Kindness/Helpfulness:
Can I Help? By S. Harold Collins (helpfulness)

Cookies: Bite-Size life Lessons by Amy Krouse Rosenthal (character)

Feelings/Emotions:
Arnie and the New Kid by Nancy Carlson

Baby Faces (DK Publishing)

I Feel by George Ancoma

Inside of Me I Have Feelings by Nancy Lee
Walker

Inside of Me If I Feel by Nancy Lee Walker

Today I Feel Silly And Other Moods That Make My Day by Jamie Lee Curtis

On Monday When It Rains by Cherryl Kachenmeister

Manners:
The Children's Manners Book
by Alida Allison

Hello! Good-bye! by Aliki

I'm Sorry by Gina & Mercer Mayer

It's Mine by Gina & Mercer Mayer

It's Mine! by Leo Lionni

Manners Can Be Fun by Munro Leaf

Miss Spider's Tea Party
by David Kirk

Perfect Pigs
by Marc Brown and Stephan Krensky

Say Please by Virginia Austin

Someday We'll Have Very Good Manners by Harriet Ziefert

What Do You Do Dear
by Sesyle Joslin

<u>Why Does That Man Have Such A Big Nose?</u> by Mary Beth Quinsey

Songs

Emotions/Feelings:
If You're Happy And You Know It

Friendship:
Make New Friends

The More We Sing Together

Manners:
Please and Thank You Magic Words

Use Your Manners

You are My Sunshine

Games & Activities Understanding Self and Others:
All About Me Activities

1. Develop a book about your child's like's and self:
   - Portrait
   - Age and birthday
   - New home address
   - Existing family
   - New Family
   - Phone number
   - Favorite color
   - Favorite things
   - Pets
   - Favorite foods

2. Create a book about their new family:
   - Portrait or picture
   - Family members
   - Pets
   - Likes and favorite foods
   - Family expectations

3. Create a daily picture activity schedule.
4. Develop routines and house rules together.
5. Label children's drawers with the clothing signs and pictures.
6. Label rooms around the house with the word and sign language.

Caring:
Respect Mother Earth
Materials: trash bags, recyclable items, gloves.

Have the children label bags of various items that can be recycled (plastic, glass, bags, aluminum, newspapers, etc.). Talk about other items that they can recycle (batteries, tires, etc.). Have the children sort through a couple bags of items to fill the bags they labeled. Check the bags with the children as they sit in a circle and talk about some of the different items that are made recycled material. What effect does this have on the earth? Have the children wear gloves and collect trash nearby. Have them sort it into their bags. Put the rest in the trash. Talk about what happens to the trash (off to the landfill, some items may degrade in months or years, while others will never degrade). What effect does this have on the earth?

Trash Sort (responsibility, respect, community)

Materials: empty, clean, plastic, glass, and metal containers; newspapers, grocery bags, markers, work gloves, trash bags.

Label each grocery bag with an appropriate picture or name to identify the type of items to be placed in the bag. Place all the items on a table and all the children to sort them into the correct bags.

Wear work gloves and collect litter on a neighborhood walk. Sort the items after returning to the classroom.

Empathy: Crying Baby

Materials: Picture of a crying baby.

At circle time talk about what children think the baby may be crying about. Ask each child to come up with an explanation as to what would make the baby cry. Then ask each of them what they could do to stop the baby from crying. Ask them what else someone might do if they were upset, wanted something, or were not feeling well? Talk

through each of the scenarios the children present to explain the crying and have them come up with ways to solve the problem for the baby.

Labeling & Understanding Others Feelings:

Materials: Feelings felt and felt board.
Role play different situations and ask children how it would make their friends feel if_(going through multiple scenarios of situations). Have them create what that would look like with the feelings felt. Have each of the children to make a face that shows how they think it would look.

Have them look at the child next to them to see what faces they are making.

Different & Similar

Materials: Dolls or stuffed animals
Talk to the children about the difference between various dolls (boy, girl, color, height, hair, etc.) or stuffed animals. Have each of them come up with something different. Then have them talk about the differences between them and their friends. Close by talking about how we are all unique and different and that is part of what makes us special.

Helping Someone Feel Better

Materials: none.
Begin by asking the children questions as follows:

- How can you tell how someone else is feeling? How can we tell if they are mad? What could we do to help someone who is mad?
- How can we tell if they are sad? What could we do to help someone

who is sad?

- How can we tell if they are hungry? What could we do to help someone who is hungry?
- How can we tell if they are happy? What makes us happy?

Listen to their answers. Help them come up with ones if necessary.

Ask them how they are feeling?

Key in on facial expressions that accompany feelings. Have the children practice making these faces and looking at one another to see what others look like when they are experiencing these emotions.

Note: For preschoolers you can add The Golden

Rule. "Do to others as you would want them to do to you." Talk about how this means treating others as you like to be treated.

Feelings/Emotions:
Emotions Circle Card Game

Sit in a circle. Give your child two paper plates. One with a sad face and one with a happy face. Have them choose between happy and sad as you read emotion sentences. Here are some examples to choose from:

- *"I dropped my ice cream on the ground"*
- *"I got a new toy."*
- *"I got to eat my favorite food."*

*See enclosed half sheet Emotions Card set in the accompanying Social Emotional Activities Workbook.

Face Pass

This game has 2-20 players
Go over the emotion signs. The players are arranged in a close circle. They can be seated, if desired. The leader starts by making a funny, dramatic, or unusual face, and then the leader passes this face to the next person, who must copy the

face. Both then turn to show everyone else in the group the faces made. The second person then creates a new face to pass to a third person, following the same direction.

This continues around the circle until everyone has a turn. It's amazing what people will come up with, and even more so when a very serious person comes up with the most ridiculous face. If someone is having trouble coming up with a face to pass, let them know that they can say and sign "Next," with the option to make a face at the end if they wish. This will prevent embarrassment about participating in the game. On the other hand, you can encourage (not force) them to try, because it is great fun. Doing something quickly without thinking is probably the best way to cope. Talk about different emotions some of the faces represented and use the signs for those emotions.

Feeling Faces

Materials: paper, markers, pencils, crayons, scissors.

Cut out blank faces that the children can fill in for themselves. Discuss different feelings, while teaching them the signs for those words. Have them fill in the faces for the last week as to how they felt each day or fill one out each day (overall).

Feelings Felt Board

Make a simple felt body with a face. The body should look similar to that of a gingerbread man. Make several circular faces that fit the body. Each face should portray a different feeling. Put the body and all the faces on the felt board. Have the children come up one at a time to choose the appropriate face for the emotion signed. Have the child tell when/why they had similar feelings. Have all the children from each of the signed emotions together as a group.

Feelings Lotto

Materials: paper, marker, clean contact paper, construction paper.

Draw six circles on a piece of paper. Draw a happy face, sad face, angry face, afraid face, silly face, and surprised face and label each with the emotion (or other emotions, if desired). Make one copy for each child. There are three different things you can do with the faces:

Leave some sheets whole, cut up others to make a Lotto game.

Cut out pairs of each feeling, mount them on construction paper, laminate or cover with clear contact paper, and use them to play concentration.

Use the page as a tool to help children clarify how they feel. The teacher can ask "Which face looks like how you feel?" and then have them circle and color that faces. Discuss.

My Emotions (emotions)

Sit in a circle. Teach your children signs for the following emotions angry, happy, love, sad, tired. You can show pictures of each emotion. Have the children respond to the appropriate sign to each of the following statements:

- *"There is a lightning storm outside, how do you feel?"*
- *"My brother took my favorite toy out of my hand."*
- *"My friend is coming to play with me."*
- *"Mommy gives me hugs."*

Friendship: Dancing Balloons

Materials: 9-inch round balloons, permanent markers, large sheets of colored tissue paper, masking tape, music.

Give each child a blown-up balloon. Have the children make faces on the balloons using permanent markers. Make a body out of the tissue paper. Using masking tape, attach one corner of the paper to the balloon knot, wrapping the tape around it several times. While music plays, the children can dance with their new dance partner by throwing the balloons in the air and catching them or laying the balloons across their extended arms and revolving around and around. They can change partners by changing balloons.

Firefly Game

Form a circle and turn down the room lights.

Let one child pretend to be the firefly by holding the flashlight. The firefly shines the flashlight around and stops the beam on another child and recites (while the rest of the group signs):

Firefly, firefly, oh so bright! Firefly, firefly shines at night
Firefly, firefly, what a sight!
I see _in the night!
The firefly has to fingerspell the name of the child they spotlighted and the child becomes the next firefly and we begin again until everyone has had a turn to be the firefly.

Fishing for Friends

Materials: Polaroid camera or pictures of each child from home, scissors, metal lid, stick, string, magnet, wash tub or other large container (optional).

Take a Polaroid picture of each of the members of class or have them bring in a picture from home (good time to do this after school pictures come out). Glue each picture to a lid. Have the children sit in a circle and sign their names one at a time so that all can see how they are spelled/finger spelled. Spread the pictures out on the floor or have a large washtub. Have each of the children take turns fishing (with a pole that has a magnet tied to it) for a classmate. The person then gives the fishing pole to the person who they picked. Have the children return the "fish" they have caught. Once the children have played 10 rounds or so as a single group, then pass out a few more fishing poles to speed along the fun. Add the extra poles by picking those who do not seem to be getting picked by the other children.

Friendship Map

Materials: butcher paper, map, crayons, markers, or colored pencils; toy cars, trucks and figures.

Have the children sit around a very large piece of paper (roll or butcher block). Show them a real map and how it is used. Have them each fingerspell their name for the whole group to see. Then ask them each to draw a house in front of where they are sitting, on the paper. Have each of the children take turns drawing a line (road) from their house to that of a friend. Label each of the roads for the child that drew them. Let them play with and add more features to their map. They can play with cars, trucks, figures, etc. Post on the wall when they are done or roll up for them to play with on another day.

HUG A BUG

Materials: music and music player.

Play fun dance music. When the music stops, the children find one of several others to hug until the music resumes, then they start dancing again.

The Good Friend List

Materials: marker and poster paper.

Ask the children what they think a good friend is? What do they do to show they are a good friend?

Make a list and post. Come back to time and time to revisit what they came up with and to see if the children have any other ideas of skills or traits that can be added to the list.

That's Me!

Materials: none.

Each child gets to talk during their turn to say something they like. Everyone who also likes the same thing yells, "That's me!" Children learn quickly about others in their class with similar likes.

Gardening:

Gardening has many benefits to the flowering of young children's social and emotional development (pun intended). Participating in the process of gardening from soil preparation to picking the "fruits" of their labor evokes so many of the character qualities that culminates in social-emotional maturity including: responsibility, cooperation, diligence, patience, caring, creativity, determination, and being thorough. Having a small garden accessible to children in early childhood programs, whether in the classroom or a designated outdoor plot, invites them to engage in each step involved in growing plants, whether fruits, vegetables, or flowers. Children greatly enjoy learning the hands-on procedures in gardening from 'working the dirt', planting seeds, watering, and weeding; to eventually, picking and enjoying what they've grown.

Extensions to the practical learning include: having the children keep a journal (dictated and with their own drawings) to track the progress of their plantings; or following the continuing journey fruits and vegetables take once they leave the garden, through books, videos, or a field trip to see how it is processed from garden, to factory, to markets or restaurants, to the table for people to eat and enjoy! The garden also furnishes built-in lessons in the scholastic areas of: concepts–colors, recognition and selection; math–counting, measuring, sequencing and order; science–life-cycles of plants, and eco-conservation.

Gardens also offer a special delight to the five senses: seeing, hearing, touching, smelling, and tasting!

Bulbs

Materials: bulbs (daffodil, crocus, tulips, hyacinth, amaryllises, etc.), shovel, gardening gloves (optional), compost or shredded leaves, ground limestone, slow-release fertilizer, water.

Be sure to check the planting instructions that come with your bulbs. Each has its own planting depth and a season which should be planted (usually you plant bulbs in the fall). Daffodils and tulips should be planted 6 to 8 inches deep, while crocuses are 4 inches. A good rule of thumb is to plant each bulb a depth of three times the largest diameter of the bulb. The best and easiest way to plant bulbs is to layer them in the garden. Dig a hole the size of a dinner plate, about 9 inches deep. The soil removed from the top of the bed is the most nutritious, thus "topsoil." You want this rich soil on the bottom where the bulbs can use it, and the soil mixed with compost or shredded leaves and a sprinkling of ground limestone. This provides a nutritious bed for the roots of the bulbs. Place six daffodils equally spaced in the whole, pointed side up. Cover the daffodils with more soil until the hole is 4 inches from the top. At this level, plant 10 to 12 grape hyacinths, also equally spaced and pointed side up. Again cover with soil and plant snowdrops on top at 2 to 3 inches from the top hole. Fill in the remaining space, firm the soil by gently pressing it down with your foot, fertilize with a slow-release fertilize such as Holland Bulb Booster and gently water. Add more soil if needed.

The bulbs bloom at different times, each only showing above the ground for a few months. They are compatible and provide a beautifully display when planted closely together. Layering bulbs also works or trench planting. You can make a crazy quilt pattern or even write your names in different colored bulbs. Once planted, the bulbs return year after year to bring pleasure to everyone.

Garden on the Go

Materials: containers such as old shoes, coffee cans, baby carriages, wheelbarrows, wagons, or buckets (as long as it can hold soil and water and can easily be moved, ones with drainage holes work best); soil, shovel, seeds, water, scissors (optional).

Use your imagination when choosing a container. Just about anything can be used! Fill your container with soil and plant your seeds. Water your seeds (if you have a container without drainage holes be careful not to over water or your seeds and plants may "drown" and die).

You can plant grass seeds in an old show or rubber boot. It will grow fast and can be trimmed into designs with scissors for fun. You can keep containers indoors or outdoors, depending on your container and the plants. Move your gardens wherever you want!

Grow a Bulb in Water!

Materials: clear glass vase with a narrow neck and wide rim, water, large bulb (hyacinth, daffodil, jonquil, Scarborough lily, Cuban lily etc.).

Fill the glass vase with water up to its neck. Place the bulb in the top of the vase so it sits comfortably in the neck. It mist not slip down too far. Make sure the water is just touching the bottom of the bulb. Put the vase in a cool, dark place until the roots are well developed. Bring the vase into a brightly lit room and the bulb will send up green leaves (shoots). In time, it will flower.

Growing Potatoes and No-Dig Garden

Materials: potato, knife, saucer.

Cut the potato into several pieces with at least one eye on each piece. The eyes is a small hole on the surface of the potato and this is where the potato will send out shoots. Lay the pieces on a saucer and place the saucer in a dry, airy, dark spot. Check your potato pieces every week or so. In time the eyes will from buds that will then form shoots. When the shoots are about 4 inches long, they are ready to be planted. Plant the potato pieces outside in your no-dig garden or regularly in your vegetable garden.

No-dig Garden

Materials: very large plastic pot (at least 20 x 22 inches), well-aged lawn clippings or straw, compost, fertilizer (pelletized poultry manure or bloodmeal and bonemeal), newspaper.

Cut out the bottom of the pot. Place the pot in a sunny position out in the garden. Put a thin layer of newspaper (3-4 sheets) at the bottom of the pot and cover with a layer of straw and a layer of compost. You can also use decayed leaves. Sprinkle a good handful of fertilizer over the layers. Continue making these layers until the pot is filled. Make small holes in the top of the materials; plant your potato pieces and cover them up again. Harvest your potatoes in 4-5 months: turn your pot upside down and remove the potatoes from the roots of the plants.

Herbs in Pots

Materials: clay garden pots, nontoxic paint to decorate pots (look for one that won't wash off), paintbrushes, potting mix, slow-release fertilizer, trowel, water, watering can, herb seeds, labels for plants (write name of plant on popsicle stick).

Decorate your pots with paint. Allow to dry. Place potting mix and some of the fertilizer granules into the pots, using the trowel, and press down firmly. Water. Sprinkle a little seed on the top of the mix. Place a thin layer of potting mix on top of the seeds. Press firmly and water again. Add labels or you might forget which herb is which pot. Place your pots in a sunny position. Keep moist and the seed will germinate and grow. Be sure to water regularly, as water will evaporate more quickly in pots than in the ground.

How to Grow Strawberries

Materials: small potted strawberry plants (buy from a nursery or collect runners from a friend who has strawberry plants growing), a sunny spot in the garden with well-drained soil, compost, liquid fertilizer, bloodmeal and bonemeal fertilizers, shovel, water.

Choose a spot in the early spring to make a garden bed for your strawberries. They grow well in a sunny position where the soil is well drained and not always soggy. Dig the bed by loosening the topsoil and adding any organic matter: old decaying leaves or any compost. Sprinkle over some fertilizer: a cupful of bloodmeal and bonemeal will get strawberries off to a good start. Leave the bed for 1-2 weeks without planting. Allowing it to rest this way means you can dig out any weeds that grow. Plant your runners 18 inches apart. Water well and keep moist until the plants become established. Feed the plants once a month with a fertilizer that dissolves in water, once your strawberry plants begin to flower. This will encourage the fruit to be large and sweet.

How to Make a Vegetable Garden

Materials: paper or cardboard, pen, rope or hose, shovel; animal manure, compost, or complete fertilizer; rake, sticks, string, vegetable seeds or seedlings, vegetable labels, hose or watering can, fertilizer, gardening gloves (optional).

Draw an outline of your garden on a large sheet of paper or cardboard and mark in where you are going to place each type of vegetable. Refer to your plan when planting. Choose a sunny position away from large trees. Choose a location with good drainage that receives at least 6 hours of sunlight a day. The spot should be level, protected from gusty winds and close to a water faucet or hose connection. Mark the outline of your plot or bed with a piece of rope or hose. If the area is lawn covered, remove the grass. Dig over the top of the soil to a depth of 8 inches. Add animal manure, compost, or complete fertilizer and allow the soil to rest for several weeks. Pull out any weeds that begin to grow. Just before planting, dig the bed again to break down the soil into small, crumbly particles. Rake the bed so the soil is even. This will make a fine seedbed for your vegetables.

Supermarkets and garden centers have stands displaying all types of vegetable seeds and seedlings. Have a good look and decide which varieties you would like to grow. On the back of the seed packet, you will find information about the best time to plant, how deep to place the seeds, how far apart to space seeds, as well as how to look after your plants.

Place a stick in the ground at each end of a row. Stretch a piece of string between the two sticks spanning the length of the row. The stretched string forms a straight line to follow when you plant. At one end of the row, place your plant marker. It is sometimes hard to remember what you have planted where, especially when using seed, so it is a good idea to label your vegetable bed as you are planting. Do not crowd plants by planting seeds too close together. Crowding weakens the plants and results in fewer vegetables or flowers. Roots need room to spread and grow. Large seeds are easy to space correctly as they can be transferred to your hand and placed one at a time to the depth and

distance advised on the packages. Tiny seeds are more difficult to spread. One way to plant them is to fold a piece of paper in half, empty your seeds into the crease, and let them fall slowly out of the crease onto the seed bed. You can also mix tiny seeds with sand and then spread them, but to be successful make sure you use more sand than seed.

If the seed is to be grown in clusters rather than lines, toss the seed thinly in each section, cover them with recommended depth of fine soil and firm gently. Water with a fine spray to prevent the seeds from washing away. Keep the soil moist until the plants have emerged and become well established (7 to 21 days, depending on the type of seed, the condition of the soil, and the weather). When the seedlings grow large enough to handle, thin them to the spacing recommended on the seed packets for each variety. Go out to your garden area regularly to see if your plants are wilting or if the ground is dry. Give them a drink if they need it. Fertilize regularly by scattering a complete fertilizer around the ground close to the plants. This is called broadcasting. You could also use a fertilizer that dissolves in water.

Look on the back of the package and it will tell you the correct amount of fertilizer and water to use. Spoon the fertilizer into a watering can, add the proper amount of water, and stir until the fertilizer is dissolved. Pour it around the roots and over the leaves of your plants. You can prolong the harvest and increase the production of most flowers or vegetables by picking them regularly.

Watering tips:

- Don't water plants every day. First, look at them to see if they are wilting, or feel down in the soil to see if it is dry.

- Water early in the morning or late in the afternoon when the temperature is cooler, so that less water is lost in evaporation.

- When hosing, stand about 3 feet away from the plants.

- Don't have the water pressure too high or the plants may be damaged, and the soil disturbed, by the jet.

- Only water the area around the plants: not the fences or walls by swinging the hose around. Water the ground and the plants rather than the leaves.

- Give your plants a thorough soaking when they need it rather than little drinks now and again. Water your potted plants with a small watering can.

- Feel whether the potting mix is dry before watering.

- When dry, give your plant a good soaking, until water drips out of the hole(s) in the bottom of the pot.

- Water vegetables and annuals more often than other plants. This is necessary because they have a small root system supplying moisture to a large leaf area.

Plant an Oasis

Materials: gardening gloves, watering can or hose, shovel, trowel and other gardening tools; young trees, shrubs, seedlings, or seeds.

Find a spot that needs flowers or a tree, like an empty dirt patch between the squares of a sidewalk or a weedy stretch by the side of a road. Get permission to plant there. Learn what kinds of plants will do well in the spot that you've picked. Prepare the soil for planting. Dig out any weeds you find, loosen the soil with a trowel or shovel, and moisten it to make a nice, comfortable home for the plants to move into. Mix some ground-up vegetable scraps into the soil. As they rot, they will provide nutrients for your plant to feed on. Dig a hole that's slightly larger than the plants you want to put into the ground. Now the only trick is to put the green side up and the brown side down. Fill in plenty of soil around each plant, mashed down firmly so it doesn't wiggle around. If you are planting seeds, follow the instructions on the package.

Take care of anything you plant as it grows. Pull out any weeds that appear, and make sure the soil stays moist. You can also water greenery that you didn't plant; it will be most appreciative.

Starting Seeds Indoors

Materials: peat pot, peat pellet, seed 'n start kit, eggshell halves, or household containers such as old milk containers, plastic and paper cups, or clay pots; seeds, planting mix, dome or plastic bag, tray or spray bottle.

Starting seeds indoors extends, by weeks, the length of time flowers bloom in the garden. Seedlings transplanted into the warming, frost- free garden soil flower much faster than seeds planted directly into the garden at a later date. For all seeds, timing is important. You can plant a fast sprouting seed such as a sunflower inside just for the pleasure of watching it grow. But if you want to transplant it to the garden where it can grow tall enough to flower, plant the seed indoors about six weeks before the last frost leaves your area. If you plant seeds too early, they will grow weak and spindly, held in a pot too long before they can be planted in a frost- free garden. One way to start seeds indoors is to plant them in saved eggshell halves. When they're ready to transplant, just gently squeeze the shell to crush it and set the whole thing, plant, shell and all, into the garden. The shell actually provides some nutrients, too.

For planting in peat pots, plant three seeds in each peat pot and later thin to one seedling per pot. Plant the peat pot in the garden with the soil level inside the peat pot beneath the surface of your garden. Carefully loosen or tear the sides and bottom in a few places to allow roots easy access to your garden's soil. Remove any of the pot's rim that protrudes above the soil level to prevent the molded peat from acting like a wick that draws water up, and dries out the roots.

If using pots to plant, purchase a planting mix for best results. It should not contain weed seed and should provide balanced nutrition. Fill planting containers to ½ inch of the top of the container. Saturate your planting mix so it is damp but not soggy. Let the excess water run out the bottom, but don't let the container sit in water. If your soil is too wet, your seed roots will rot. Let the planting mixture set a half hour or so until it becomes evenly moist before planting your seeds. Once the seeds are in the planting mixture, cover them with a dome, or enclose the entire unit in a clear plastic bag to preserve the moisture. The bag should not be allowed to touch the soil and can be easily held up with a plant marker or stick to create a tent. The tent acts like a greenhouse, keeping the air and soil moist and warm. Set it in a warm place out of direct sunlight. If the seeds require light, a windowsill exposed to sunlight five or six hours a day is ideal. Check daily to assure your seeds are evenly moist. The best method of watering is to set your containers in a tray of water for a half hour until they absorb as much water as they can hold. If you are watering from the top, spray with a very delicate soft spray. Don't over water or let water sit in puddles on top of the seed. When seedlings appear, remove the plastic bag, and place the plants in light to avoid stem rot. If you set the plants in a window, turn them daily so they will grow straight as they reach for sunlight. An ideal seedling is straight, deep-rooted and bushy.

Sunflower House (farm & garden) Materials: sunflower seeds, morning glory seeds, shovel, garden gloves (optional), string.
Prepare the soil for planting. Mark out the side of your sunflower house for planting. You can make your house any

size you want, be sure to leave an opening for a door. Plant sunflower seeds about 1 foot apart. If you wish for your sunflower house to have a morning glory roof, plant morning glory seeds at the same time as the sunflowers. Plant the morning glories outside the rectangle (or whatever shape your house is) of sunflowers. Plant extra sunflowers and morning glories, then weed out the excess when they reach a few inches in height. The sunflowers will show themselves first. As the morning glories grow, they will twine clockwise around and up the sunflowers. It is important to remember clockwise direction while training the morning glories at the beginning of their ascent. If you twist them counter-clockwise, they will slowly unwind and rewrap themselves clockwise. When the sunflowers are about four feet high, tie string under their heads and stretch it from one sunflower to another directly across from it, then back again to its neighbor simulating a "cat's cradle." The string provides the morning glories a roof framework to grow along. The sunflower house can be decorated. You can place table and chairs or a blanket or beach ground inside the house when playing.

Tepee Garden

Materials: fast growing vines (scarlet runner bean, Jack-be-little pumpkin, morning glory, moonflower, love-in-a-puff), sunflower seeds, flower seeds such as marigolds and strawflowers, radish seeds, shovel, bamboo poles, rope, trellis netting (optional), large plastic garbage bag (optional), towel or small rug (optional).

Prepare the garden soil. After the danger of spring frost, sow the seeds directly in the garden where they are to grow, following the instructions on each seed package. Position the tepee in the middle of the garden or wherever you wish. To make the tepee, set bamboo poles in the ground and tie together at the top with rope. A trellis netting can be wrapped around the poles to make it easier for the vines to climb and cover the tepee structure. Plant the vines evenly spaced, a few inches apart, around the outside tepee structure (scarlet runner beans and Jack-be-little pumpkins work the best). When seedlings emerge, they can be thinned to the distance recommended on the seed packets.

Plant sunflowers on the backside of the tepee to "stand guard" over the garden and grow seeds that can be harvested for bird feed or roast for snacks. In the front side of the garden plant flowers and radishes. A large plastic garbage bag can be laid on the ground inside the tepee to keep weeds from growing. Later when the vines are covering the tepee and the children want to play inside it, a towel or a small rug can be laid inside.

What to Grow in Your Garden

It is best to choose vegetables you enjoy eating and that are easy to grow. Snow peas, beans, lettuce, radish, pumpkin, zucchini, Swiss chard, carrots, tomato, Chinese cabbage, sweet pepper, and green shallots (spring onions) will be relatively easy. Fast-growing, leafy salad greens such as Romaine lettuce as well as Chinese cabbage would also be good beginners' choices. When choosing what to plant, keep in mind the idea of companion planting. This means growing next to each other certain plant varieties that do well together by nourishing each other and/or by discouraging harmful insects. Marigolds are well known insect inhibitors and make a fragrant, colorful garden border. Here are some good companion plants: tomatoes and basil or parsley; tomatoes and carrots; lettuce and carrots; radishes and cucumbers; carrots with peas and lettuce; corn and pumpkins; zucchini with beans or radishes; parsnips and potatoes with peas and beans. Here are instructions for growing several easy to grow vegetables.

Beans

Materials: shovel, gardening gloves (optional), bean seeds, liquid fertilizer.

You can select a dwarf or bush bean variety such as "Tendercrop," that only grows to 20 inches, so that you will not need to stake the plants. Sow the seeds in warm soil in early spring. Make a shallow furrow (or a small trench) 1.5– 2 inches deep. Place each seed 4 inches apart, along the furrow. Cover lightly with soil and press down firmly. Water gently. Wait until your seeds start sprouting and then feed every 2 weeks with liquid fertilizer. Bean seeds do not like direct contact with fertilizer at the planting stage. Pick your beans in 8-10 weeks. They are crunchy and delicious when eaten right after harvesting!

Remember, the more you pick the more you get, because the plant's energy moved from maturing the fruit to making more flowers that will develop into more beans.

Carrots

Materials: shovel, gardening gloves (optional), carrot seeds, dry sand (optional), wood ash (optional), fertilizer.

Sow carrot seed at any time of the year, except for winter. The tastiest carrots are usually sown in early spring. Soil that has been deeply worked and has had all the stones and sticks removed so the roots will grow straight are best. Good drainage is also important to prevent rotting and disease. Wood ash spread over the surface and raked into soil will provide a good source of potassium for sweeter-tasting carrots. The seed is quite small. Mixing it with some dry sand first makes it easier to sprinkle evenly over the bed. Plant the seeds directly in the spot you want to grow them: carrots don't like being transplanted. Choose a sunny position. Cover the seeds lightly with soil. Water your carrots regularly. If the soil goes from wet to dry all the time, the carrot roots will crack and split. Fertilize only after the carrots begin growing so the roots will be well shaped. Carrots, like all the other root crops, may grow into funny shapes if the soil has had fresh animal manure added to it at planting time. Pull your carrots in 4-5 months when they are fully grown. Smaller carrots will be ready for harvest in 60-70 days.

If you leave some carrots in the garden over the winter, they will produce lovely flowers and seeds for planting the following spring.

Pumpkins

Materials: shovel, gardening gloves (optional), pumpkin seeds (collect it yourself from a pumpkin or buy it in a packet from a plant nursery), large peat pots (optional), fertilizer (bloodmeal and bonemeal or soluble).

Pumpkins do not transplant well and should be seeded indoors if at all possible. If not, place in good-sized peat pots and transplant pots and all. If you have short summers, soak seeds overnight before planting. If using a peat pot, leave the pot in a warm spot until the seedling emerges. When the seedling has grown 2 leaves, it is ready to be transplanted. Plant the seedling still in the peat pot, in your vegetable patch. Water regularly, especially in dry weather. Fertilize monthly with bloodmeal and bonemeal or a soluble fertilizer, once the plant begins flowering and while it is bearing fruit. Leave the fruit on the vine until it is fully mature (16-20 weeks). Harvest when the vine dies and the fruit stalk turns brown and withers. Leave about 4 inches of the stalk attached to the fruit when cutting and it will keep better.

Radishes

Materials: shovel, gardening gloves (optional), radish seeds, liquid fertilizer.

Choose radishes if you are growing vegetables for the first time. They are quick to grow and do not need much care. Sow the seeds at any time of the year, except during winter in cold climates. Be sure the soil is free of rocks and stones that can cause misshapen roots. The usual way to plant radishes is to sow them in double rows 6 inches apart with a foot between each set of rows. Sow seeds 1/3 inch deep with three seeds per inch of row. Cover lightly with a sandy soil mixture. Water gently. Within a week, seeds will have germinated and the leaves of the seedlings will be showing. Be sure to water regularly. When the plants are half grown, thin them so there are 12 to 18 plants per foot of row. Apply liquid fertilizer every 2 weeks to keep them growing quickly. Slow growth makes radishes taste bitter. Pull the radishes in 4-6 weeks when they are ready to eat.

Zucchini

Materials: shovel, gardening gloves (optional), zucchini seeds, fertilizer.

Select a zucchini variety that suits your needs. Most zucchini plants are space hogs as they have huge leaves and grow on long spreading vines. If you don't have a large area, choose a bush type, such as Gold Rush: it will grow into a compact bush and produce a lot of fruit with a golden yellow skin. It is even small enough to grow in a large container. Sow the seed any time in spring, at a depth of ½ inch. Space seeds 3 feet apart, if you are planting more than one seed. Feed and water regularly. Zucchini love water and fertilizer. Harvest in 7-8 weeks when the zucchini are ripe.

Gentleness: Blowing Bubbles

Outdoor activity if at all possible. Have each of the children pair up with a container of bubbles. Have them teach each other how to fingerspell their names. Have one of the children blowing the bubbles while their partner tries to catch them.

Have the teacher use a large bubble wand to produce great big bubbles for the children to try to catch. **Bubbles** Materials: clean pail, 1 cup dish washing detergent (Joy or Dawn work best), 3-4 T. glycerin from pharmacy (optional), 10 cups clean cold water, large spoon, plastic bubble wands.

Pour the water into the pail and add the liquid detergent and the glycerin. (Glycerin makes the bubbles more durable.) Lightly stir and skim off any froth with a spoon. Give a plastic wand to each child and demonstrate how to blow bubbles.

Using a bowl placed in the water table reduces the amount of spills and cleanup, as well as frustration when children accidentally spill their bubbles.

Set up a bubble obstacle course in the classroom where the children blow bubbles as they walk along a path. The path could include such exercises as blowing a bubble through a hula hoop, walk backwards, catching bubbles, and so forth.

You can also purchase a giant bubble wand for outdoor play.

Manners Activities:
Role Modeling

Being an example of good manners is the best way to teach good manners. Use signs for "please", "thank you" and "you are welcome." Routinely sign "yes please" or "no thank you."

Reading

Sign a story regarding manners with your child. For example, ask your child to sign the word "please," every time you read the word "please" from a book. Greetings -- Use signs to greet the children and use the signs for manners.

Manners

Routinely say "yes" "please" or "no" "thank you" in sign.

Polite or Impolite?

Materials: three teddy bears.
Explain the definitions of polite and impolite. Emphasize courtesy and following the Golden Rule. Set up a table

with three teddy bears. Explain that the bears are having tea and a snack. Ask them to raise their hands and tell you if they are being polite or impolite.

Give enough examples that you can call on all the children. Examples:

- How are you today?
- Hello.
- Give me some cookies!
- Pass the cookies, please.
- Thank you for inviting me.
- May I have some sugar, please?
- Give me the sugar!
- Wiping her hand on her shirt (motion).
- May I have a napkin, please?
- Tell me the time!
- What time is it?
- Give me some more tea!

- May I have some more tea, please?

- Get it yourself!

- I would be happy to pass you the tea.

- Please join us next time.

- Thank you, everything was wonderful.

- You should have bought more cookies!

Let's Play Tea Party

Materials: tea set (child size or full adult size) including cups, saucers, spoons, teapot, sugar bowl, creamer pitcher; table and chairs, real or pretend tea, water, juice or other liquid; real or pretend cake, cookies, crackers, or small sandwiches; plates, napkins, table cloth and decorations (optional); stuffed animals or dolls as additional guests.

Prepare a small table for a tea party with enough chairs for each person or toy invited. Cover the table with a tablecloth, or set out place mats. Set out the tea set, napkins, plates, and whatever other items you might have for the tea party. One person is the host and the others are guests. The host is in charge of pouring tea and serving the guests (you can take turns on being the host). Use polite conversation and manner signs (thank you, more please, welcome, etc.).

Say Something Nice

Materials: soft ball that is easy to catch (such as Nerf or foam ball).

Have everyone sit in a circle. Then either throw, pass, or roll a Nerf ball to someone else in the circle and give that person a compliment. No repeats to persons are allowed until everyone has had the ball and a compliment. Ask the group to try to give different compliments each time. That's it! It feels good for someone to acknowledge you!

The Talking Wand

Materials: wand or toy microphone.

Discuss with the class that it is impolite to interrupt while someone else is talking. To help remember that, only the person who has raised their hand and is holding the wand (or microphone) may talk. That way, everyone can hear and understand what is being said and can practice being good listeners.

Conflict Resolution:
Mad Hatter

Talk to your children about appropriate ways they can express their emotions when they are angry or unhappy. Teach them the signs for these emotions. Write down each of their answers on an index card. Draw or cut and paste a picture that represents their actions. Put all the cards into a hat. Explain that when they are angry or upset they can draw a card from the hat and do what it says or use their signs to express their signs in a positive manner. The Mad Hatter should be available during free play times.

Relaxation:
Relaxing Images

Talk to the children about seeing things with their eyes closed (visualizing). Can you see when you dream? What sorts of things do you see? Can you hear or taste or touch or feel anything? Have the children sit in a circle. Tell them to lie down and close their eyes. Ask them to picture in their minds the detailed common item you describe.

- I see something round and white. It is too high for me to touch. It is brightest in the night. It can change shapes from a sliver to full circle.
- It can affect the tides here on earth. The moon.
- I see something red. It is sort of round and can be eaten. It grows on a vine, rather than a tree. I eat it in my salad. A tomato.
- I see something green. It is cold blooded and scaly. It has four legs and can walk on land, as well as swim in water. It has a tremendous tail. It has a long snout and lots of teeth. An alligator.
- I see something metallic and shiny. It has many keys, but no doors to open. It can remember whatever I tell it and it can teach me a lot. I also play games with it and chat

with people from faraway places. A computer.

When you are through with each item, tell the children to open their eyes and ask them each to sign the key words as they describe what they pictured in their heads.

Taking Turns:
Co-operation Playdough

Materials: 2/3 cup salt, 2 cups flour, 1/3 cup vegetable oil, 2/3 cup water, few drops of food coloring, large bowl, large spoon (for each group making dough).

Divide class into groups of 3-6. Discuss turn taking asking what it means and when we take turns. After talking about the importance of taking turns, tell the class that they are going to make play dough but they have to take turns when making it. Allow the children to take turns adding, mixing, and stirring the ingredients together. (Mix dry ingredients first and then add oil, water, and food coloring). When finished, divide dough into parts and give to children to play with. Be sure to reinforce turn taking during other activities and try to plan other activities where children can practice turn taking (snack, games, sharing time, etc.).

The Great Predictor

Materials: costume turban (or one made from wrapping a towel around the head) with a large feather plume.

The children take a turn at being "The Great Predictor," that is, they wear the turban and answer questions the teacher asks. Each questions begins with "Oh, Great Predictor..." and then follows with a question designed to get the children thinking about consequences and rewards for their actions. Be sure to have questions relevant to the classroom/child. Here are some sample questions:

- What will happen if we get upset and hit or push someone?
- What will happen if we share?
- What will happen if we interrupt others? What will happen if we leave our toys or things out?

Toilet Paper Pull

Materials: colored or patterned toilet paper.

On each table place a roll of colored or patterned toilet paper. Without being told why, the group is instructed to pass the roll around, and each person may take as much as he wishes from the roll. When every person has taken from the roll, they are told they must tell one fact or interesting piece of information about themselves for each square they have torn off. For some, this may mean only one or two things—some may have to relate 25!

Crafts
Calming: Jewel Floats

Materials: large clear plastic bottles with caps, baby oil or water, food coloring (optional), waterproof tape or hot glue gun, old jewelry, glitter, scraps of foil, small plastic toys.

Have children work in small groups or individually. Fill the bottles with baby oil or water, add food coloring if desired. Have the children cut up foil scraps and drop them in the bottle. Add glitter, old jewelry, and small toys. Put the cap securely on the bottle and tape or glue it closed. While repeatedly turning the bottle upside down, the children can search for and track particular objects. Place the floats so that they are accessible to the children in the room. The jewel float is a relaxing and soothing toy. You can make floats to fit any theme being studied (ocean, color theme, animals, etc.).

Emotions:
Emotions Art Activity

Give children a piece of paper and have them draw a card with a face on it showing their emotions.

Friendship: Balloon Friends

Materials: 8-9 Inch round balloons, cardboard, yarn, colored construction paper, scissors, glue, markers.

Talk about what makes friends special. Then cut out the feet of the friend they are making on the cardboard. Cut a slit into the center of the feet and insert the knot on the bottom of the balloon. Children can make and decorate the faces as they see fit.

Friendship Bracelet

Materials: Baker's clay, small plastic straws (coffee), tempera paint, small brushes, string. (Baker's clay can be purchased or made by mixing 2 cups of flour, 1 cup of salt, adding water until it forms a dough consistency.)

Explain that the purpose behind the making of this bracelet is to put together as many beads from different friends in the classroom as they can. Have the children roll out small beads from the clay. Each child should make at least 10 beads. Poke a hole through the beads with the straw. Allow beads to dry for 2 days or more. Have the children paint the beads as they see fit. When the beads are dry have the children exchange beads with the other children. They should only have one of their own beads left. String the beads to form the bracelets.

Gentleness:
Feather Face Painting

Pair up the children. Have them sit directly in front of one another. Have them teach their sign fingerspelled names to their partners. Explain that they are going to take turns painting their partners faces with feathers (do not include the eyes). First the eyebrows, then the forehead, then the hair, then the cheeks, then the nose, then the lips, then the chin and finally the neck. Be sure you emphasize painting softly. There are no actual paints involved with this activity.

Pussy Willow Pictures

Materials: pussy willow branches, light blue construction paper, brown crayons, glue sticks, small cotton balls, gray finger paint (tempura), small bowls.

Have the children touch the pussy willow branches to see how soft they are. Begin by having the children draw the branches of the pussy willow on the light blue construction paper. Then have them glue on the cotton balls.

Older children can use gray finger paint to paint the buds, instead of using cotton balls. Pour some of the paint into small bowls, just a little so as to barely cover the bottom. Have the children press down on the paint in the bowls with their index finger and them use their finger to make the bud on the picture. Repeat until you have enough buds.

My Little Ocean

Materials: 2-liter clear plastic bottles with caps, baby oil, water, food coloring, duct (or other waterproof) tape, small-medium size plastic jewels, glitter, strips of foil, small sea shells, sand, small plastic sea toys.

Begin by putting 1 part baby oil to 3 parts water. Then add food coloring, if desired. Then put in varying amounts of each materials inside the bottle (sand, sea shells, sea toys, glitter, strips of foil, jewels). Then put cap on tightly and tape with duct tape.

Manners:
Sneeze Pictures

Materials: paper, glue, crayons or markers, facial tissue.

Discuss the importance of covering one's mouth when coughing or sneezing. Explain that when we cough or sneeze we can spread germs that can make others sick. Have the children draw and color a face (for young children a pre-drawn face to color is a good idea). When they have finished have them glue a piece of tissue paper to the nose to serve as a reminder of what to do when we cough or sneeze.

CHAPTER 3

CARING CENTERS

Doll Care Activities for Young Children

Doll Care provides immeasurable benefits to young children's social and emotional development. Participating in the process of caring for another, whether it is a person or animal, teaches so many of the character qualities that culminates in social/emotional maturity; namely: responsibility, cooperation, diligence, patience, caring, creativity, and determination. Having a doll caring center accessible to children in early childhood programs invites them to engage in process of learning to love and take care of that baby doll. Children greatly enjoy learning through play how to feed, change, potty train, bath, put down for a nap, and otherwise care for their baby doll. The doll care center also furnishes built-in lessons in the scholastic areas of: Concepts--colors, recognition and selection; math--counting, measuring, sequencing and order; and science--life-cycles. Doll care experiences offer a special delight to the senses – seeing (watching their and others care of the doll(s)), hearing (listening to others interactions with the doll), touching (feeding, caressing, hugging, bathing, dressing, and potty training), smelling (clean and dry vs. wet/dirty and stinky), and tasting (pretend sharing food).

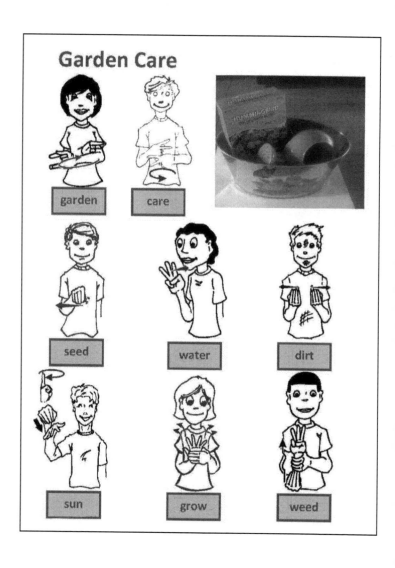

Garden Activities for Young Children

Gardening has immeasurable benefits to the flowering of young children's social and emotional development (pun intended). Participating in the process of gardening from soil preparation to picking the "fruits" of their labor evokes so many of the character qualities that culminates in social/emotional maturity; namely: responsibility, cooperation, diligence, patience, caring, creativity, determination, and being thorough. Having a small garden accessible to children in early childhood programs, whether in the classroom or a designated outdoor plot, invites them to engage in each step involved in growing plants, whether fruits, vegetables, or flowers. Children greatly enjoy learning the hands-on procedures in gardening from 'working the dirt', planting seeds, watering, and weeding; to eventually, picking and enjoying what they've grown. Extensions to the practical learning can be: to have the children keep a journal (dictated and with their own drawings) to track the progress of their plantings; or to follow the continuing journey produce takes once it leaves the garden, through books, videos, or a field trip to see how it is processed from garden, to factory, to markets or restaurants, to the table for people to eat and enjoy! The garden also furnishes built-in lessons in the scholastic areas of: Concepts–colors, recognition and selection; math–counting, measuring, sequencing and order; science–life-cycles of plants, and eco-conservation. Gardens offer a special delight to the five senses–seeing, hearing, touching, smelling, and tasting!

Growing flower seeds - Requirements: pot, soil, seed, water, and sunlight. Add approximately 6 cups of soil in a flower pot container burying the seed, and water every day, placing the pot where the sun shines on it.

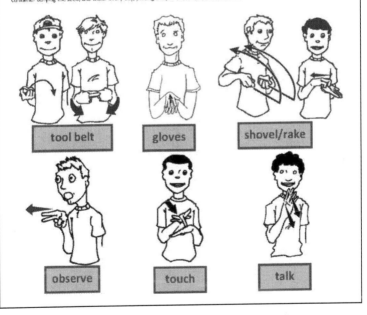

tool belt

gloves

shovel/rake

observe

touch

talk

Puppy Activities for Young Children

Animal Care provides immeasurable benefits to young children's social and emotional development. Participating in the process of caring for another, whether it is an animal or person, teaches so many of the character qualities that culminates in social/emotional maturity; namely: responsibility, cooperation, diligence, patience, caring, creativity, and determination. Having a puppy caring center accessible to children in early childhood programs invites them to engage in process of learning to love and take care of that animal. Children greatly enjoy learning through play how to feed, water, bath, brush, pet, talk with, teach tricks to (roll over, sit, lie down, etc.), and otherwise care for their puppy. The puppy care center also furnishes built-in lessons in the scholastic areas of: Concepts–colors, recognition and selection; math–counting, measuring, sequencing and order; and science–life-cycles (1to 7 years). Puppy care experiences offer a special delight to the senses – seeing (what size, shape, and color are different dogs), hearing (barking and other dog sounds), touching (petting, hugging, and grooming), smelling (60% of a dog's brain is dedicated to smell), and tasting (pretend sharing food).

play   love   walk

run   sit   teach

CHAPTER 4

SONGS & ACTIVITIES IN SIGN LANGUAGE TO PROMOTE SOCIAL -EMOTIONAL LEARNING

Feelings Song
(Sing to the Tune of Twinkle, Twinkle, Little Star)

I   have   feelings (point to self)

So do you (point to children)

Let's   all   sing about a few.

I am happy (smile).

I am sad (frown).

I get scared.
(Wrap arms around self and make scared face).

I   get   mad
(make a fist and shake it or stomp feet).

I   am   proud   of   being   me
(hands on hips, shoulders straight, smile)

That's a feeling   too,   you   see.

I   get   mad
(make a fist and shake it or stomp feet).

I   am   proud   of   being   me
(hands on hips, shoulders straight, smile)

That's a feeling   too,   you   see.

I   have   feelings
(point to self)

You   do,   too
(Point to children)

We just sang about a few.

Please and Thank You

(Original Author Unknown, Illustrations Copyright©2002 Time to Sign, Inc.)

Please   and   thank you

Please   and   thank you

magic   words   magic   words.

Everyone   should   **use**   them.

Everyone   should   **use**   them

Everyday   **everyday.**

Everyday -
swipe hand
across the
cheek 3 times.

If You're Happy and You Know It

(Traditional, Illustrations Copyright©2002 Time to Sign, Inc.)

If **you're**   **happy** and you **know** it, clap   your hands. (clap, clap)

Repeat

If **you're**   **happy** and you **know** it,   **your**   **face** will surely **show** it.

If **you're happy** and you **know** it, clap **your hands.** (clap, clap)

If *you're*   *sad*   and you   *know* it,   *say*, "boo, hoo." (pretend to cry)
Repeat

If *you're*   *sad* and you *know* it,   *your*   *face* will surely *show* it.

If *you're sad* and you *know* it, **say**, "boo, hoo." (pretend to cry)

If *you're*   *angry* and you *know* it, stomp your feet. (stomp, stomp)

Repeat

If *you're*   *angry* and you *know* it,   *your*   *face* will surely *show* it.

If *you're angry* and you *know* it, stomp your feet. (stomp, stomp)

If **you're**   **happy** and you **know** it, clap   your hands. (clap, clap)

Repeat

If **you're**   **happy** and you **know** it,   **your**   **face** will surely **show** it.

If **you're happy** and you **know** it, clap your hands. (clap, clap)

Simon Says "Feelings"

Play Simon says with the children substituting feeling phrases for the usual directions. Also, change the name as each child takes a turn from Simon to the speaking child's name. For example, say: "Michael says, look happy." In between commands you can ask them questions about those feelings, such as "What makes you feel happy?"

CHAPTER 4

ROLE-PLAYING SIGN LANGUAGE CARD SET

I dropped my ice cream cone on the ground. I feel...

sad   angry/mad

I accidentally broke my friend's toy truck. I feel...

sorry   sad

I got lost in the big store   all by myself. I felt...

scared   confused

My school friends are coming to my birthday party. I feel...

happy   excited

We are going to play my favorite game today. I feel...

happy   excited

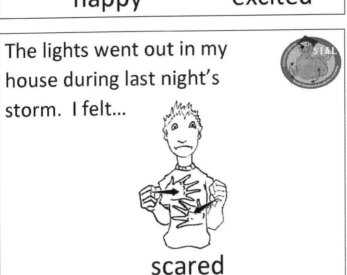

The lights went out in my house during last night's storm. I felt...

scared

My school friend took my
toy I was playing with.
I felt...

sad   angry/mad

We are going on a field trip in
school today. I feel...

excited   happy

My friend got to go to the
fair and I didn't. I feel...

jealous

I helped my friend clean
up the blocks. I feel...

helpful   proud

I wear my backpack to school all by myself. I feel...

proud

I did not understand what the teacher said. I feel...

confused

I made my mom a beautiful card for her birthday. I feel...

helpful   proud

I hurt my friend's feelings by taking their toy. I feel...

sorry   sad

CHAPTER 5

SOCIAL-EMOTIONAL LEARNING MINI-POSTERS WITH SIGNS

ABOUT THE AUTHOR

Dr. Michael S. Hubler, Ed.D. is the Executive Director of EC-LEARN, a not-for-profit organization dedicated to helping early childhood educators, children, and families with their developmental and educational needs and issues. He earned a doctorate of education degree from Regent University with a specialization in the Social-Emotional Learning of Young Children and a masters' degree from Radford University, where he was a Graduate Teaching Fellow.

He has directed non-profit and governmental service organizations for over 25 years. He was the Executive Director of the Outstanding Minority Education Institution (Florida, 2005). He was also named Citizen of the Year twice (Brevard County, Florida, pop. 560,000, 2010 & 2013) and he was the Executive Director of the Humanitarian Organization of the Year (Central Florida, 2014).

He has published over 50 early childhood education books and curriculums and has trained thousands of educators nationwide in the social-emotional learning of young children and how they can create a positive-preventive environment for the betterment of both the children's behavior and learning, as well as to enhance the work lives of their teachers.

Questions, or if you would like to learn more about SEL trainings call (321) 726-9466.

53165109R00070

Made in the USA
Columbia, SC
14 March 2019